A Visit to WALES

Chris Oxlade and Anita Ganeri

Heinemann Library
Chicago, Illinois

Customer Service 888-454-2279
Visit our website at www.heinemannlibrary.com

Designed by Ron Kamen and StoreyBooks
Originated by Dot Gradations Ltd.
Printed and bound in China by South China Printing Company

07 06 05 04 03
10 9 8 7 6 5 4 3 2 1

Library of Congress Cataloging-in-Publication Data
Ganeri, Anita, 1961-
   Wales / Anita Ganeri and Chris Oxlade.
      v. cm. -- (A visit to)
Includes bibliographical references and index.
Contents: Wales -- Land -- Landmarks -- Homes -- Food -- Clothes -- Work-- Transportation -- Language -- School -- Free time -- Celebrations --The arts -- Fact file.
   ISBN 1-40340-967-6 (Library Binding-hardcover)
  1. Wales--Juvenile literature. [1. Wales.] I. Oxlade, Chris. II. Title. III. Series.
   DA708 .G36 2003
   942.9086--dc21
                              2002007417

Acknowledgments
The author and publishers are grateful to the following for permission to reproduce copyright material: pp. 5, 6 Corbis; pp. 7, 8, 10, 11, 12, 18, 19, 20, 21, 25, 29 Peter Evans; p. 9 The Photolibrary Wales/David Williams; p. 13 Food Features; pp. 14, 23 The Photolibrary Wales/Steve Benbow; pp.15, 27 Trip/M. Barlow; p. 16 Wales/Simon Regan; p. 17 Trip/P. Rauter; p. 22 John Walmsley; p. 24 Action Plus; p. 26 The Photolibrary Wales/Kathy De Witt; p. 28 Collections/Ken Price.
Cover photograph of Conway Castle in Gwynedd, reproduced with permission of The Photolibrary Wales/Harry Williams.

Every effort has been made to contact copyright holders of any material reproduced in this book. Any omissions will be rectified in subsequent printings if notice is given to the publisher.

Some words are shown in bold, **like this.** You can find out what they mean by looking in the glossary.

Contents

Wales

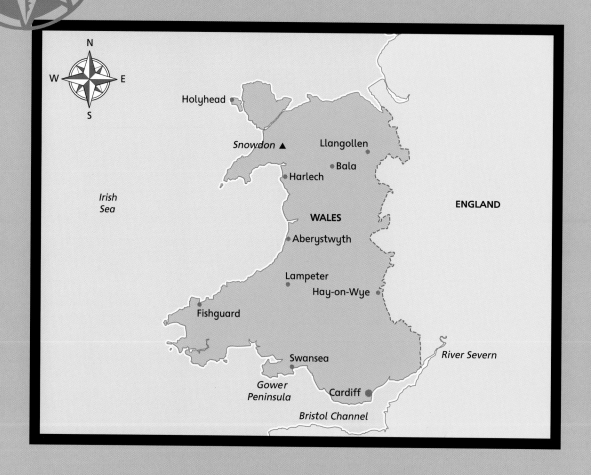

Wales is a country in the United Kingdom. It is also part of a group of islands called the British Isles. Things and people from Wales are called *Welsh*.

The **capital** city of Wales is Cardiff.
This city is on the southern **coast** of
Wales. Cardiff has many old buildings,
including the castle shown here.

Land

Southern and middle areas of Wales are green and hilly. The Gower **Peninsula** in southern Wales sticks out into the sea like a finger. It has wide, sandy beaches.

Many vacationers visit the beaches of northern Wales. **Inland** from the **coast** are the mountains of Snowdonia. The highest mountain is called Snowdon.

Landmarks

Wales has many beautiful castles. Most of them were built by King Edward I. He ruled England and Wales over 700 years ago.

The Millennium **Stadium** in Cardiff is the largest sports stadium in Wales. It can hold many people. A sliding roof covers the playing field when it rains.

Homes

Most of the people in Wales live in the cities of Cardiff and Swansea, in southern Wales. Some live in apartments like these. Others live in houses.

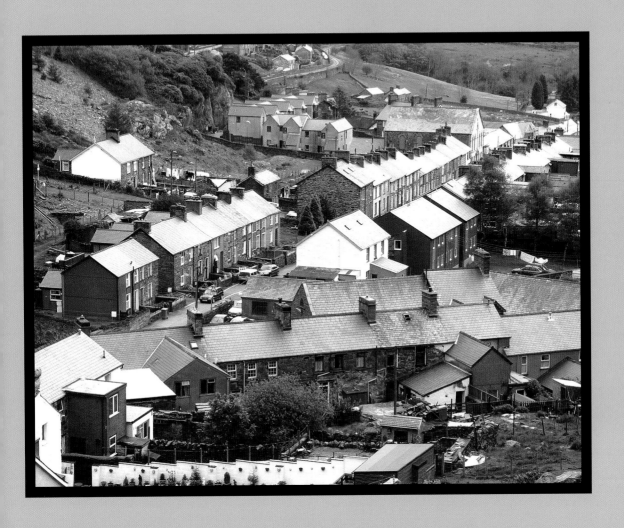

Many Welsh people used to work in coal **mines**. Today, most of the mines are closed. **Terraced** houses like these were built to be homes for the miners.

Food

Laverbread is not bread at all. It is a type of seaweed found on the **coast** of Wales. It is cooked in salty water and is usually served on toast.

These are Welsh cheeses, cakes, and breads.
The loaf at the bottom is called *bara brith*,
which means "speckled bread."

Clothes

Young people in Wales wear clothes such as T-shirts, sweatshirts, jeans, and sneakers. Clothes from sports **designers** are very popular in Wales.

These women are wearing the **traditional** Welsh **national costume**. Today, people in Wales only wear these costumes for special occasions, such as Welsh music and poetry festivals.

Work

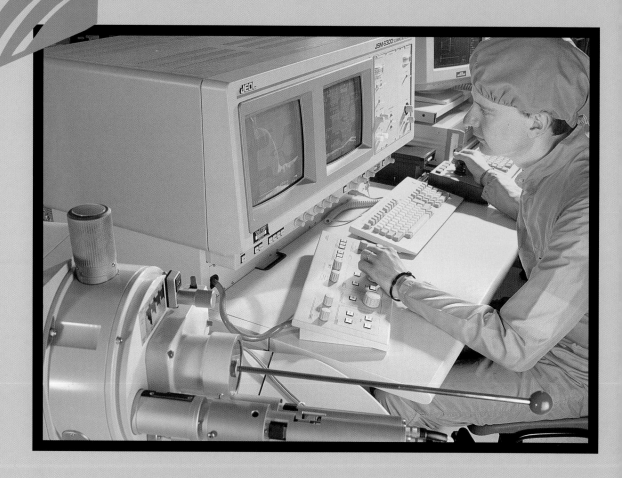

Many Welsh people work in **service industries** such as banks. Other people work in factories, making things like cars, televisions, and computers.

Most of the countryside in Wales is farmland. Farmers keep sheep and cattle in the hills. Sheepdogs help round up and control the sheep.

Transportation

The Severn River separates southern Wales and England. It is very wide. Two huge bridges over the river connect the two countries.

Holyhead is a **port** on the island of Anglesey in northern Wales. **Ferries** run from Holyhead to other places. Trains carry people from Holyhead to the rest of Wales and England.

Language

Most Welsh people speak English. Some people speak Welsh as well. Welsh is mainly spoken by people living in northern and western Wales.

In Wales, signs are written in Welsh and English so that everybody can understand them. The Welsh word for Wales, *Cymru*, is used in the top arrow.

School

In Wales, children go to **nursery school** when they are four year sold. They start regular school when they are five years old. This class is in a city school in southern Wales.

This is a small school in a country town.
Students in Wales learn to speak and
write in Welsh and English.

Free Time

Welsh children play sports such as **rugby, football,** and **netball.** Rugby is the **national sport** of Wales. The boys in this picture are playing rugby.

People in Wales enjoy going to the **coast** or **sightseeing** on the weekends and during school vacations. Wales has lots of beautiful countryside for walking or pony riding.

Celebrations

Saint David is the **patron saint** of Wales. Welsh people wear the **traditional** symbols of the leek or the daffodil on Saint David's Day.

Welsh festivals are called *eisteddfods*. The International Eisteddfod is held every July. Singers, dancers, poets, and musicians come from all over the world to perform.

The Arts

Music is very popular in Wales. Many towns and villages have a **traditional** choir of men. They sing at concerts and local events.

The town of Hay-on-Wye in southeastern Wales is famous for its bookshops. It has many shops selling used books. A book festival is held there every summer.

Fact File

Name   Wales is the English name for the country. The Welsh call it Cymru.

Capital   The **capital** city of Wales is Cardiff.

Languages   Welsh people speak both English and Welsh.

Population Three million people live in Wales.

Money   Money is called pounds sterling. Its symbol is £.

Religion   Many Welsh people are Christians, but there are also people of other religions, such as Muslims, Sikhs, Hindus, Jews, and Buddhists.

Products   Wales has a lot of sheep farms producing wool and meat. It produces a lot of iron and steel. Tourism is important, too.

Welsh words you can learn

Cymru (say: CUm-ree)   Wales

bore da (say: boreh-da)   good morning

hwyl fawr (say: hooil-vowr)   goodbye

plis (say: plis)   please

prynhawn da (say: praown-da)   good afternoon

Yr Wyddfa (say: ear-withva)   Snowdon

Glossary

capital	most important city
coast	where the edge of the land meets the sea
designer	person who plans what something will look like
docks	where ships are loaded and unloaded
ferries	passenger ships that go back and forth from one place to another
football	English word for the American game of soccer
inland	land that is away from the sea
mines	pit or tunnel where minerals are dug up
national costume	clothes that people used to wear in the past in a particular country
national sport	most important sport in a country
netball	team game based on running, jumping, throwing, and catching
nursery school	place where young children begin learning
patron saint	saint who is said to look after a country
port	where ships arrive, carrying people and goods
peninsula	piece of land with sea on three sides
rugby	game similar to American football
service industry	business that provides services for people
sightseeing	visiting interesting or beautiful places
stadium	place where many people watch sports or events
terraced	houses that are joined together in a line
traditional	something that has been done the same way for many years

Index

More Books to Read

Bell, Rachael. *United Kingdom*. Chicago: Heinemann Library, 1999.

Britton, Tamara L. *Wales*. Edina, Minn.: ABDO Publishing Company, 2002.

Heinrichs, Ann. *Wales*. New York: Children's Press, 2003.

The y Draig Goch (Red Dragon) is the flag of Wales.